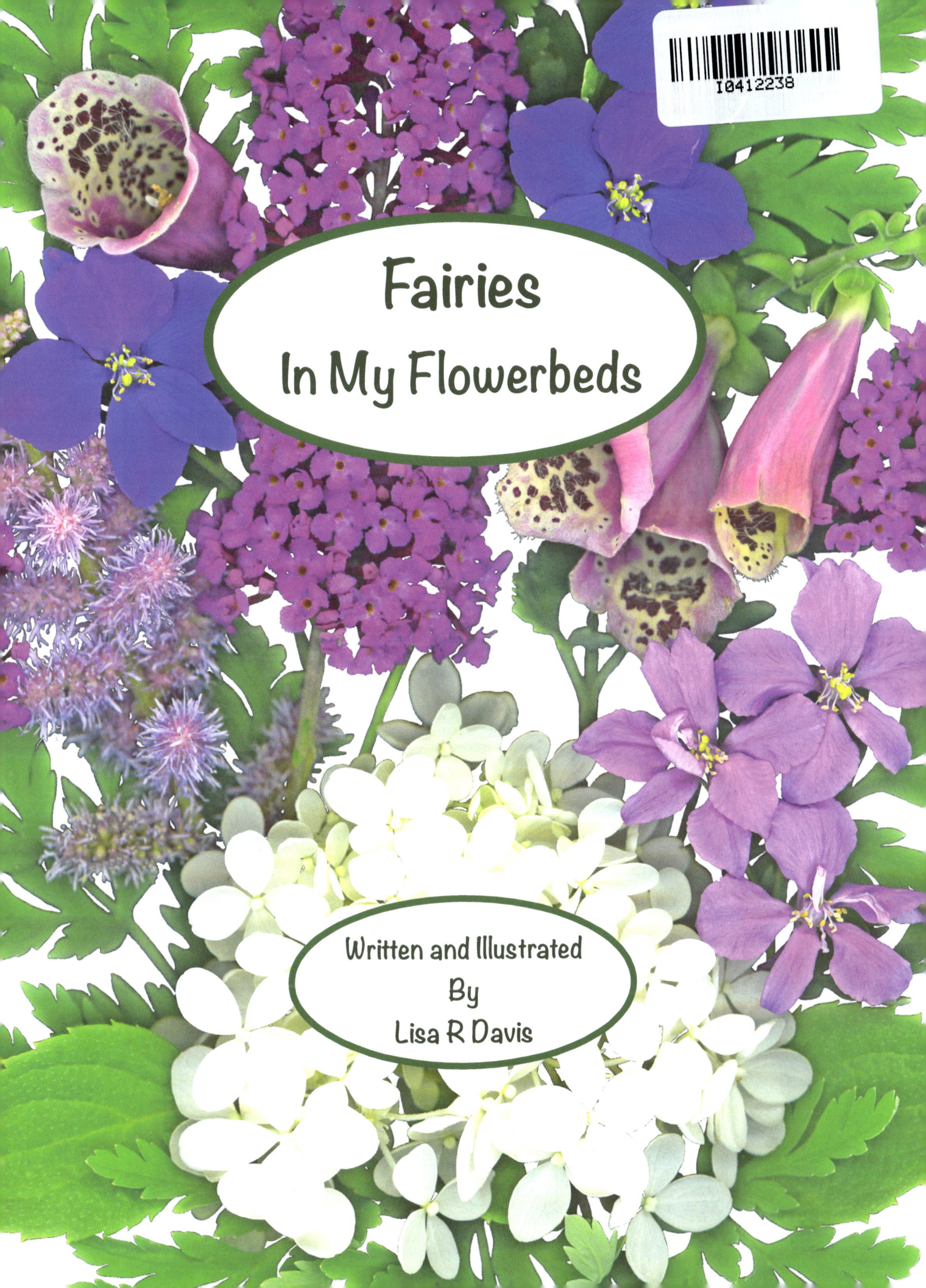

# Fairies In My Flowerbeds

Written and Illustrated

By

Lisa R Davis

For my mother, Carole and my daughter, Teagan
(the nut really doesn't fall far from the tree)

ISBN-10: 1482605112
ISBN-13: 978-1482605112

# A Surprise

I've worked in gardens many years
for, oh, so many hours
that's because I care so much
for all my lovely flowers

And then one day I saw appear
before my very eyes
a sight I'd never seen before
a really big surprise!

It was a warm and lovely day
the middle of the spring
what I saw filled me with joy
and made me want to sing

Do you know just what it was
that could surprise me so?
Can you guess just what I saw
that set my heart aglow...

## A Bleeding Heart Fairy

I saw a tiny fairy
with a soft, pale purple gown
she had two pigtails on her head
that pointed up, not down

I was so surprised to see her
that I couldn't speak a word
I'm sure my mouth hung open
and made me look absurd

Fairy: a bleeding heart, a rhododendron blossom and columbine petals
Flower: bleeding heart

## Springtime In the Garden

After spotting that one fairy
I started seeing more
as if that pink-haired fairy
had opened up a door

That door led into Fairyland
so come along with me
through a springtime garden
and I'll show you what I see...

## Heather Primrose

I see a fairy I call Heather
she's a very welcome sight
she adds color to the garden
after all the winter white

Although her name is Heather
that's not what she's made from
she just really loves that plant
it is her closest chum

Neither seems to mind the cold
when the sun is brightly shining
they both know that winter's hold
is rapidly declining

Fairy: a primrose blossom, petals and bud with crocus leaves, holding a staff of heather

Flowers: heather

## Mary Myrtle Daffodil

Mary Myrtle is her name
she's yellow, green and white
she's mostly clothed in daffodils
a very lovely sight

She wears the tip of myrtle spurge
upon her tiny chest
I long and wait for her return
and then feel very blessed

She likes to dress up fancy
she's a ray of bright sunshine
each spring I am so thrilled to see
this fairy friend of mine

Fairy: three varieties of daffodils, and a single blossom of myrtle spurge
Flower: daffodil

11

## Corey Columbine

He's a tiny fairy baby
dressed in a one-piece suit
I really want to hug him
just because he is so cute

I adore his purple hands
and teensy curling feet
the white cap on his little head
always smells so sweet

Fairy: a columbine blossom, a lily-of-the-valley blossom, a chionodoxa seedpod, holding a forget-me-not staff

Flowers: columbine

13

## Fairy Godmother Magnolia

She looks like she grants wishes
is there magic in her hand?
Can she make your dreams come true
with just one swift command?

Fairy: a saucer magnolia, tulip petals, pulmonaria buds, an uncapped acorn,
and a spring anemone blossom
Flowers: saucer magnolia and tulip

15

## Tamsyn Tulip

This fairy's name is Tamsyn
she cheered me up one day
I was feeling sad and blue
she chased that right away

She laughed and did a silly jig
then threw both arms out wide
"Ta-dah!" she shouted joyfully
"Bravo!" I replied

Fairy: a partially-opened spring anemone, a tulip blossom and petals,
a bleeding heart blossom, and clematis stems with leaf buds
Flower: snowdrop anemone

17

## Welcome Summer

Brother Sun shines stronger
so the fairies change their clothes
I wonder what they'll think to do
with a winsome summer rose…

## Piper and Pepper Rosebud

The peachy little rosebud twins
are always full of charm
they often prick my fingers
but never do real harm

Fairies: opening rose blossoms, and rose petals, buds and stems
Flower: sprig of roses

## Baby Boo Hydrangea

This tiny fairy baby boy
has wings and clothes of blue
why, even his appendages
are just that very hue

He's clothed in small hydrangea parts
a flower, large and fair
seeing him just makes me think
of a much-loved teddy bear

Fairy: hydrangea petals and stems, with a cosmos bud and calyx
Flower: hydrangea

23

## Gracie Green
## A Ginkgo Girl

Ginkgo trees have leaves like fans
that flutter in the air
when I looked up, I saw this girl
a sight, I'm sure, quite rare

From head to toe she was all dressed
in clothes bright emerald green
my heart grew happy when it saw
this unexpected scene

Fairy: the leaves, stems, and fruit of a ginkgo baloba tree
Twig with leaves: from a ginkgo baloba tree

25

## Giselle Clematis

Giselle is dressed in ruffles
she loves her fancy clothes
and 'specially likes the slippers
that cover up her toes

Her closet is the garden
when it's filled with blooming flowers
she tries on soft, bright petals
for many fun-filled hours

The splendor of the blooming things
just do delight her so
surrounded by their beauty
her heart can't help but glow

Fairy: cosmos petals, a cosmos bud, part of a clematis blossom, mallow petals, and impatiens seedpods

Flower: clematis

## Rowan Gaillardia

He's a kingly looking fellow
with that crown upon his head
he doesn't feel like royalty
just regular instead

If he is called "Your Highness,"
he will laugh out long and loud
he finds it quite amusing
'cuz he's humble and not proud

His heart is filled with joy
he is generous and so kind
you may call him Rowan
for that he does not mind

Fairy: gaillardia blossom, petals, stems, and seed-head
Flower: gaillardia

## Fiona Cosmos

Take a nice long stroll outside
if you are feeling down
you might see Fiona there
then you'll no longer frown

Fairy: a cosmos bud and an opening cosmos blossom, petals and stems
Flower: cosmos

31

## Welcome Fall

Again it's time for changes
as cool breezes start to blow
I wonder what the fairies wear
in autumn's golden glow…

## Penelope Sunflower

My angelic, graceful fairy friend
so feminine and yellow
whenever she draws close to me
she makes me feel so mellow

This radiant sunshine fairy
so elegant and bright
whenever I spend time with her
my heart is filled with light

Fairy: sunflower petals, cosmos petals, a poppy seedpod, and part of a Japanese anemone blossom

Flower: sunflower

## Lizzie Lou Lace

Are you a meadow fairy?
Are you found among the trees?
Do you play beside a country road?
You do just as you please

You like to play and laugh and tease
you're full of nice surprises
and are ready to have lots of fun
no matter what arises

Fairy: Queen-Anne's-lace seed-heads, a crab apple, maple leaf stems,
and a woodland ground cover leaf
Twig: the fruit and leaves of a crab apple tree

## Sawyer Sumac

This fairy's name is Sawyer
he has sumac wings of red
I like the jaunty acorn cap
he wears upon his head

His tunic's from a tulip tree
so stately and quite tall
it turns a lovely yellow
sometime later in the fall

He has trousers from a sunflower
that strong and sturdy stalk
with azalea buds for hands to hold
and feet so he can walk

Fairy: sumac leaves, a tulip poplar leaf, an acorn, azalea twigs and buds, and sunflower stalks

Twig: staghorn sumac

## Sienna Seedpod

The colors seen in autumn
cause the eyes to open wide
there is no way to name them all
though many times I've tried

Orange, yellow, brown and green
just have so many hues
when asked to pick my favorite one
there was no way to choose

Scarlet, crimson, carmen
are all names for shades of red
although there must be many more
the thinking hurt my head

So I just sat back and gazed
and bathed my brain in beauty
when suddenly out popped this girl
a charming little cutie

Fairy: a maple leaf, rhododendron leaves, a hibiscus calyx, and a nigella seedpod and stems
Leaf and seeds: maple tree

41

## Welcome Winter

Most plants now are sleeping
Old Man Winter's come around
roots and seeds remain quite snug
tucked safely underground

But near my house there is a bush
that stays around all year
can the fairies use it
or do they disappear…

## Holly Berry

With wings dark green and shiny
and cheeks quite red and bright
on dreary days in winter
she is a welcome sight

Fairy: leaves and fruit of European holly, a primrose blossom with part of its calyx,
and crocus leaves

Twig: from a holly bush

## Waiting For Spring

Although it may look bleak outside
remember what you've seen
for now we have our memories
till again the world turns green

47

# A note from the author / illustrator

I wear many hats, and one of those hats is that of a scanographer. Scanography — sometimes spelled scannography, also called scanner art or scanner photography — is a kind of digital photography, but instead of using a camera to capture an image, a scanographer uses a flatbed scanner. The fairy pictures in this book are created by gathering and arranging pieces and parts of my garden flowers and the plants that surround my country home. I place the plant materials face down on my scanner in a form that I imagine fairies look like. I then do multiple previews, rearranging the materials each time, until I obtain an image I can work with. I complete the figure in a computer graphic arts program.

It is a sad fact that fairies did not enter my house and lie quietly face down on my scanner to have their portraits done.

*One of my backyard gardens in early July*
*(a hardiness zone 5 garden)*

To see more fairies, flowers, and a few more garden pictures, visit me at:
www.WallflowersAndCards.com